ALL ENDS UP

ALL ENDS UP

Cartoons by S. Harris

From *American Scientist*

Foreword by Linus Pauling

WILLIAM KAUFMANN, INC.   LOS ALTOS, CALIFORNIA

Dedication

To Isaac and Albert and the rest of
the gang down at the lab.

ISBN: 086576-000-4

Printed in the United States of America

FOREWORD

It was inevitable that Sidney Harris appear in the world. Students of evolution tell us that some species of living organism develops to fill every niche. Jonathan Swift in 1751 said, "If I can but fill my Nitch I attempt no higher Pitch." We are fortunate that Mr. Harris is filling his "Nitch," because it might have been occupied by some lesser species, and that would have meant that we—scientists and laymen alike—would have been deprived of some of the joy of life.

In this, the third collection of his science cartoons to be published as a book, he continues to delight us. I remember that old dictum that "Behind every great man there stands a surprised mother-in-law"; Mr. Harris replaces the surprised mother-in-law by a great computer. He introduces plays on words—navy ants complement army ants. He reminds us that the human beings of prehistoric times, 15,000 to 100,000 years ago, or more, had as great intelligence as modern man by portraying one of them as an art critic who says to an artist, "You're truly the spokesman for your generation," and who analyzes a rock carving by saying, "The forward thrust of the antlers shows a determined personality, yet the small sun indicates a lack of self-confidence."

The critics of big industry may take a lesson from Mr. Harris's comment that the ozone layer is a threat to the fluorocarbon industry, and those philosophers who feel the cosmic significance of the Heisenberg Uncertainty Principle may be comforted by the psychiatrist's advice that you shouldn't go through life applying Heisenberg's Uncertainty Principle to *everything*.

As a critic of conventional medicine and conventional nutritional science, I am comforted by knowing that Mr. Harris's patient stopped taking the medicine because he preferred the original disease to the side-effects, and that the worm has found that an hour in the compost pile provides his minimum daily requirements of everything.

Also, as a person who dictates punctuation along with the words when answering letters or composing papers, I can easily put myself in the place of the scientist, in his laboratory, who dictates, "Eureka exclamation point."

I wish that I knew Mr. Harris's secret—the secret of creating great humor. Sometimes I look at a dozen or more cartoons in some currently popular magazines without finding one that seems to be really funny. By my criterion of humor, whatever it may be, Mr. Harris is successful about 99% of the time. This may mean only that he and I happen to think alike, but I believe that most of the readers of this book will agree that Mr. Harris is a man of good judgment, with a really sound sense of humor.

—*Linus Pauling*

"It's probably just a technicality, but is the biosphere extended to wherever we go?"

"Here's where the sales department comes in, Webb. As we continue to remove it from the gasoline, we're going to have a lot of lead on our hands . . ."

LOW-
TEMPERATURE
PHYSICS LAB

S.harris

3

"Keep in mind that, like everyone else, I use only ten percent of my brain."

"Just don't think about it. We've always been carnivorous, and we always will be carnivorous."

"My problem has always been an overabundance of alpha waves."

6

"Your old heart was fine after all. We put it back. You're the first recipient who's his own donor."

"The last I heard, Medwick was working on a model black hole in his lab."

"Now, if we run our picture of the universe backward several billion years, we get an object resembling Donald Duck. There is obviously a fallacy here."

9

"It's not the humidity—it's the thermal pollution."

"The question now is, 'How many *neutrinos* can dance on the head of a pin?' "

"I wouldn't worry. With continental drift, Africa or South America should come by eventually."

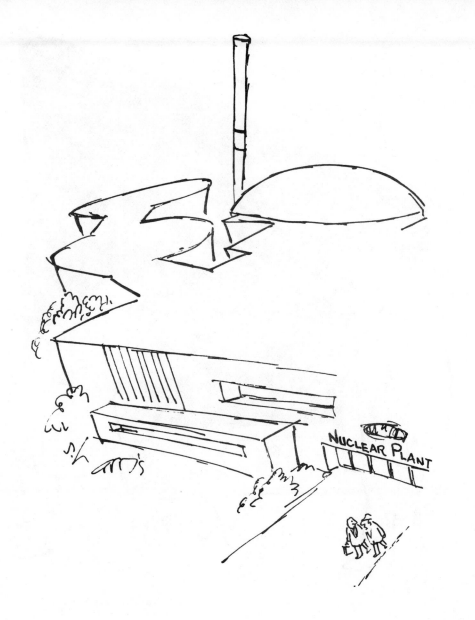

"Of course it's perfectly safe. Any accident would be in complete violation of the guidelines established by the Nuclear Regulatory Commission."

"That's *it*? That's peer review?"

"Here's one for the books—I'm a whooping crane, and I've never been counted."

"Well, Gottfried, news from the cloning front, I see!"

"A good x-ray, but not a great x-ray."

17

"It just isn't working. What shall we do?"

"Dyslexia? What's lysdexia?"

19

"Bunsen, I must tell you how excellent your study of chemical spectroscopy is, as is your pioneer work in photochemistry—but what really impresses me is that cute little burner you've come up with."

I've never understood why, in pictures of people walking downstairs the top of The stairs is at the bottom of the picture, and the bottom of the stairs is at the top of the picture.
s.harris

"All right—now convert the whole thing to metric."

"This new drug works on streptococci, pneumococci and staphylococci. Now here's where you come in . . ."

"You mean Casey's book on Hamlin's Syndrome will be out before *my* book on Hamlin's Syndrome?"

27

"It sounds like an implosion."

"If automation ever creeps into *this* place, I'm getting out."

"And as for Research and Development, Stevens—you people haven't come up with a new toxic substance in three months."

"The forward thrust of the antlers shows a determined personality, yet the small sun indicates a lack of self-confidence . . ."

"Every once in a while I just like to unwind with a little addition and subtraction."

"I wouldn't worry about it. What they do is take it *out* of the ocean, and *then* desalt it."

"He was working on a theory of entropy, and developed a severe case of it himself."

"Necessity is *usually* the mother of invention."

"Well—the moons of Mars are even *smaller* than we thought!"

"This is not what we meant, Snider, when we asked for a thorough study of the laws of gravity."

"True, the fluorocarbon industry's threat to the ozone layer may very well be serious, but the ozone layer's threat to the fluorocarbon industry is equally serious."

43

"In effect what you're doing is you're taking a big lead off third.."

"Oh, oh—Navy ants!"

"You both have something in common. Dr. Rudolph has discovered a particle which nobody has seen, and Prof. Higbe has discovered a galaxy which nobody has seen."

"It certainly becomes uncomfortable when the pollutants are up to 990,000 parts per million."

"As I read it, we're receiving a message from outer space telling us to stop bombarding them with unintelligible messages."

49

"When you're young, it comes naturally, but when you get a little older, you have to rely on mnemonics."

50

"A black hole—that's the answer to our radioactive waste problem."

"It's the latest miracle fabric: 40% Dacron, 40% Orlon, 20% recombinant DNA."

"Show that you care. Use our new pollution-free detergent, and your clothes will be the grayest in town."

"However, it's excellent pseudoscience."

"We should be thankful. What if oil and water *did* mix!"

"I'd say it was a male, 5 foot 3, 129 pounds . . ."

"But you can't go through life applying Heisenberg's Uncertainty Principle to everything."

"One advantage of living near a binary star would be a suntan in half the time."

"I find that an hour in the compost pile provides my minimum daily requirement of everything."

61

"You have a choice of three courses. You could increase speed somewhat and retain your comprehension, you could increase speed considerably and reduce comprehension, or you could increase speed tremendously and eliminate comprehension completely."

"He heard we burn it to generate electricity and we use it for landfill, so he wants to sell it to us."

"Sure, we're dealing with tiny particles, but your formula is just a *symbolic* representation."

"Do your stuff—you're on microscope."

"What with the primary mental ability test and the differential aptitude test and the reading readiness test and the basic skills test and the I.Q. test and the sequential tests of educational progress and the mental maturity test, we haven't been learning *anything* at school."

"I think we should ask Zimmer to do those experiments. He's a Capricorn."

"It's always the same thing—the sun, a few clouds, and that's it. I'd like a transfer to the night shift."

"Now that we've got *this* wrapped up,
I'd like to get into math."

"I'm firmly convinced that behind every great man is a great computer."

"A typical vegetarian problem—green lung."

"I've been trying to trace my roots, but after a couple of generations, they go off into a different species."

"Why, it must be somatotropin, the
growth hormone!"

"Don't bother Daddy now. He's singing."

"And, to round out the four basic food groups, I recommend the gnocchi de semoule avec pâté a chou—Patalina."

"Sure it's dark out here, but still they're going to be very surprised to find that it's Mercury, Venus, Earth, Mars, Jupiter, Saturn, Uranus, Pluto and Neptune."

"This could be quite controversial—a recombinant nuclear DNA sweetener."

"You'll like this flock. We do the
regular migrating twice a year, and
then we take lots of these side trips."

"You're truly the spokesman for your generation."

"You know what I hate about this place? The heavy water."

83

"Bad news. I hear we're on the endangered species list."

"Eureka exclamation point . . ."

"I don't know what it measured. The Richter scale is down there."

"There's a 60 percent chance of 20 percent acid rain and a 40 percent chance of 30 percent acid rain."

"I must say it isn't easy adjusting to a 24-second day."

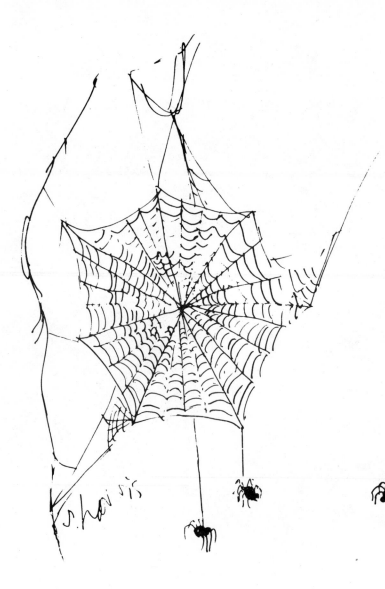

"She does invisible weaving."

"Confounded troublemaker!"

They gave me the Gauss theorem, the Gauss method for quadratics, Gaussian distribution, the Gauss eyepiece...
And I've got the Newton laws of dynamics, Newton's formula for interpolation, Newton's laws of cooling, Newton's rings...
J.Harris

"This is the part I always hate."

"As I understand it, *they're* in danger of becoming extinct, too."

"Its top speed is 186 m.p.h.—that's
1/3,600,000 the speed of light."

"My big mistake was going into cosmology just for the money."

"Remember when there was all that fuss about recombinant DNA?"

"There's *some* light coming from it. We'll just have to assume it's a dark gray hole."

"It started with the remoras, but then I picked up a catfish, a few rays, an eel, some perch . . ."

"What I had in mind was typographical elevations and circuit schematics."

"He's the typical American mouse—likes a drink before dinner, smokes a little, watches TV . . ."

102

"... and in 1/10,000th of a second, it can compound the programmer's error 87,500 times!"

"Since miniaturization began, they're even polluting *our* environment."

"... and *this* is for those drug-resistant microbes."

"Take some interferon, and call me in the morning."

"Never mind the weather report—
what's the eutrophication report.?"

"You've seen spiral galaxies, you've seen elliptical galaxies . . ."

"There goes the ecology."

"I love hearing that lonesome wail of the train whistle as the magnitude of the frequency of the wave changes due to the Doppler effect."

"If tachyons do exist, and if they do go faster than the speed of light, then I'm determined to find something that goes faster than tachyons."

PROBABILITY LABS
USUALLY OPEN 9-12
OFTEN OPEN 1-5

"Whatever happened to *elegant* solutions?"

114

"Since they stopped putting all those drugs in the feed, I've been getting a lot more colds than I used to."

"Oh, Oh—looks like a blue shift."

"It's analyzed our situation thoroughly, and has concluded that our business doesn't need a computer."

"Of course I don't look familiar—I'm recombinant."

"I won? I didn't even know there was a Nobel booby prize."

"I stopped taking the medicine because I prefer the original disease to the side effects."

"Another one uninhabited. That's three
down and several hundred billion to go."

The Artist Interviews Himself

My alter ego happened to be passing by just as I sat down to do this piece, and he offered to interview my ego. Knowing I couldn't do any better, I accepted the offer.

AE: This place is a mess. I take it you've drawn quite a few cartoons.
E: Yes, I've done several thousand over a period of more than twenty years—although it sometimes seems like twenty cartoons over a period of several thousand years.

AE: I suppose you know the reason for doing all of this, or, to paraphrase Freud, "What do cartoonists want?"
E: My original motivation, if I remember correctly, was to kill a few hours each day, but now I could do that by looking out of the window.

AE: Which, as I understand it . . . .
E: Yes, that takes up a good part of a freelancer's day. In my case I spend the first few hours of every morning looking for the mailman. If he happens to arrive early, I still look for him, hoping, I suppose, that he will reappear with tomorrow's mail.

AE: Then, I suppose, you get down to the major work of cartooning, which is drawing those little pictures.
E: Not exactly. There is always some mail to answer, some photocopies to be made, and some more windows to look through. Thus a full working day can go by without drawing, which, in any case, is so much drudgery.

AE: What else does it take to be a cartoonist?
E: Fortunately, I have two important traits: a continual case of writer's block, and a short attention span. Both can be relieved for a minute or so by coming up with an idea or caption.

AE: I've heard the propensity for humor runs in families.
E: Very likely. I've inherited a great deal from my wife, who makes sculptures which are witty and incisive, and from my two children, who are always ad libbing.

AE: I suppose you'd like to get in a plug now.
E: Well, four books of my cartoons have been published in the past few years (*So Far, So Good*, Playboy Press, 1971; *Pardon Me, Miss*, Dell, 1973; *What's So Funny About Science?*, 1977, and *Chicken Soup*, 1979, William Kaufmann, Inc.) but I don't believe any of them contain the great American cartoon. Perhaps the quest for this white whale of humor is the motivation for the whole thing.

—*Sidney Harris*